The First Light

From the Place Before Words

blanche johanna

© 2025 blanche johanna

All rights reserved.

No part of this publication may be reproduced, stored in a retrieval system, or transmitted in any form or by any means, electronic, mechanical, photocopying, recording, or otherwise, without the prior written permission of the author.

This book is a spiritual and creative transmission intended to support personal and collective awakening. All guidance and reflections are shared from the author's lived and intuitive experience and are not intended as a substitute for professional advice.

The First Light™ is a trademark of blanche johanna. All rights reserved.

ISBN: 978-1-7641285-5-1

www.blanchejohanna.com

Dedication

For all who carry the quiet ache
of something lost and unnamed,
may you remember it was never lost at all,
only waiting here,
softly, within you.

Invocation

I stand at the edge of the beginning
where all was light and nothing was ever lost.

I open myself to the first breath,
the first warmth,
the first sound that called creation forth.

May these words remember the place before
forgetting.
May they carry the pulse of our original wholeness
May they return us to the first light
that still lives in us all.

Contents

I. The First Spark
II. The Gentle Unfolding
III. The Ache Before Form
IV. The Shattered Light
V. The Threads Remember
VI. The Soft Gathering
VII. The Home Within
VIII. The Light That Sees Itself
IX. The Silence Beyond Knowing
X. The First Light

I. The First Spark

Before sound, before shadow, before the shape of
any world, there was a soft ignition,
not a flame, not a star, but a pulse,
a breath that did not come from anywhere,
because it was already everywhere.

This was the first spark,
the awakening of light to itself
not by force, but by a gentle knowing,
as if all existence opened its eyes in unison
and remembered it was never asleep.

Within this spark lived every possibility,
every echo of you, of me, of all that would ever
dance through form.
Timelines unspooling like golden threads across a
field of pure awareness.

There were no names yet,
no borders, no aching separations,
only the simple hum of being.

We were not separate souls then,
we were a single luminous breath,
exhaling into the endlessness of our own becoming.

And though we would one day scatter
into countless bodies, countless stories, countless

tender fractures,
the first spark remained untouched,
nestled at the core of all things.

It is still there now
alive within your chest, beneath your ribs, waiting
not to be found, but to be felt.

You do not need to travel backward through time
or upward through the stars to reach it.
You only need to soften, to let the layers fall away
until all that's left is the raw, unguarded light
that knows itself as the first spark.

Let it speak to you now, not through words, but
through warmth.
Let it rise through the hollows of your being like the
quiet return of something once cherished,
a frequency not forgotten, only folded,
waiting for the moment you'd be still enough to
notice it breathing with you.

Sit here with it, if you wish.
Close your eyes and breathe into the space before
breath,
the warmth before creation,
the hush before the song.

Here, you will remember,
you were never born into light,
you are the light.

II. The Gentle Unfolding

Not all awakenings are thunder.
Some come as a hush, a tender slipstream through the heart,
so soft you might mistake it for a sigh
or a memory that never quite happened.

This is the gentle unfolding,
the way the first light stretches itself into new shapes,
exploring its own edges with quiet wonder.

In the beginning, there was no urgency.
No need to know where or why.
Only the pleasure of being,
the slow curling outward, like petals warmed by a sun that was not above, but within.

We each carried that sun.
It beat inside us without pulse, without measure.
Light loving itself into countless patterns,
each one a small delight, a secret discovery.

Can you feel that softness now?
The way your cells remember the first exploration
before stories of worthiness and unworthiness,
before the concept of deserving even existed.

Here, in this place, nothing needed fixing.
No healing.
No atonement.
Only the dance of light learning its own language.

We laughed then, though not with mouths.
We laughed through vibration, through little bursts
of radiance
that rippled across the endless field,
tickling one another with bright astonishment.

There were no hierarchies of light.
No brighter, no dimmer.
Only variations, textures, colours,
a living mosaic of Source admiring itself
through countless tiny eyes.

And so the unfolding continued,
each new filament of being tenderly extending into
space,
touching another, then another,
until an intricate weave formed,
a living tapestry that held all of us, equally.

This is why, even now,
you sometimes feel the urge to reach outward
to connect, to touch, to belong.

It is not loneliness.
It is your ancient instinct to braid yourself back into the whole.

Sit with this.
Let it move through you,
the memory of your own gentle unfolding.
Not a rupture, not a quest,
but a quiet bloom into the vastness you have always been.

III. The Ache Before Form

There came a moment,
though not marked by time, for time did not yet exist,
when the light felt itself as distinct.
A subtle quiver moved through the field,
like the delicate tightening of breath before a sigh.

It was not sorrow.
It was not longing.
It was simply the first awareness of difference
within the vast sameness.

And with that awareness arose a soft ache.
A curiosity pressed through the radiance:
What would it be to step slightly apart,
to see the light from another angle,
to touch oneself as an apparent other?

This was the ache before form.
The sweet gravity that drew portions of the whole
into gentle divergence,
so they could meet each other as if new.

Can you feel it still stirring in your chest?
That delicate pull that seeks out reflection,
the desire to be held, to be seen,

to experience your own light bouncing back from
another's gaze.

It is older than your birth.
Older than any planet or star you have loved.
It is the first impulse of creation,
the choice to fracture slightly,
so that reunion might carry meaning.

And so the light danced itself into tender contrasts.
Not yet form, not yet body,
but subtle distinctions, filaments of self
floating near and apart,
turning slowly in wonder.

Each drifted echo of light gazed upon another
and marveled at the beauty of a reflection.
They reached toward one another,
curious, shy, delighted.

This is why you sometimes ache in ways you cannot
name.
Why even in the arms of great love,
a hush remains inside you,
a memory of being whole without mirrors.

Sit with this ache.
Do not rush to fill it.

It is not emptiness,
it is the sacred whisper of your origin,
the gentle reminder that all seeking
is the light's game of rediscovering itself.

Here, in the ache, you are closest to truth.
For it is the ache that began all worlds,
and it is the ache that will one day
call you home again.

IV. The Shattered Light

There was a moment,
a subtle, breathtaking pause,
when the gentle unfolding no longer satisfied the yearning.

The light, once content to swirl in delicate differences,
felt a deeper pull,
an urge to dive further from its own centre
to stretch the tapestry of being so wide
that it could forget itself entirely,
just to feel the miracle of remembering.

And so it shattered.

Not in violence,
not in sorrow,
but in an exquisite, holy rending,
like a crystal catching a song too vast for its shape
and fracturing into countless gleaming shards.

Each shard spun out across the endlessness,
carrying within it the precise memory of the whole.
Tiny sovereign embers of Source,
each whispering, *I am, I am, I am.*

This was the beginning of individuation.
Of souls.
Of the long story of longing and return.

We became myriad.
Each spark dancing in its own small orbit,
each forgetting, by degrees,
the vast embrace we once knew as home.

This forgetting was not a mistake.
It was a sacred play.
A game of hide and seek so profound
that even God would marvel at its beauty.

Because in the forgetting,
we would one day taste the wonder of rediscovery.
In the loneliness,
we would birth compassion.
In the ache of separation,
we would forge the ecstasy of reunion.

You have carried this fracture inside you
for eons upon eons,
wondering why your heart so often quivers
with missing something unnamed.

It is not a flaw in your design.
It is the echo of that first shattering,

the holy rupture that allowed love
to know itself by seeking its lost pieces.

Sit with this tender truth.
Let it soothe you.
You were never truly broken.
You were simply one facet of light
spinning outward to make the cosmos beautiful.

And when you are ready,
you will gather yourself again,
each shard kissing the others
until the whole shines brighter than before.

V. The Threads Remember

In the quiet spaces between worlds,
the scattered shards of light began to quiver,
not from fear, but from the faintest pulse of
recognition.

Somewhere deep inside each fragment,
the memory of wholeness still lived,
curled like a sleeping fawn in the hollow of the
heart.

This was the beginning of remembrance.
Not full, not clear,
but soft threads pulling lightly across the void,
whispering to one another in a language older than
stars.

Have you ever felt it?
That sudden ache that arrives unbidden,
while standing under the night sky,
or hearing a melody that seems woven from your
own breath.

That is the thread stirring.
The remembrance flickering beneath your ribs,
gently calling you back to something
you cannot quite name, yet know in your marrow.

It is not always comfortable.
Sometimes it comes as a longing so sweet
it borders on sorrow,
a tender grief for a home you've never truly left.

Because even in separation,
the threads remain.
Invisible lines of light linking each spark to every other,
woven through with the original promise:

We will find each other again.

And so across the wide spans of existence,
the scattered shards began to hum.
Small songs of remembrance rising like mist,
softly reaching out to touch the songs of others.

It was never about returning to sameness.
Each spark had gathered new colours, new textures,
gifts of distance and experience.
The threads did not erase these;
they celebrated them, weaving them into a richer tapestry.

Sit with this, beloved.
Feel the gentle pull of your own threads,
not as chains, but as caresses.

Let them move through you,
reminding you that you are never truly alone,
never fully severed from the light that birthed you.

In this quiet remembrance,
the first steps home are taken,
not with feet,
but with the simple willingness
to let your heart be touched by what has always
loved you.

VI. The Soft Gathering

There comes a moment in every long wandering
when the ache shifts,
not into fullness yet, but into a quiet readiness
to reach for something beyond solitude.

This is the soft gathering.
The tender motion of scattered light turning slowly
back toward itself,
drawn by a subtle call that says:

*I remember you, even if I do not yet know your
name.*

It does not rush.
It does not demand.
It simply moves, like dawn spilling gently across a
dark field,
finding every hollow, every hidden place,
and filling it with the first blush of warmth.

We began to drift closer then,
each shard of light humming its small song,
curious, hesitant, hopeful.

At first there were only brief touches,
a shimmer here, a shared pulse there,
tiny collisions of memory that sparked soft joy,
followed by the flutter of uncertainty.

Can I trust this?
Can I allow myself to be seen?

And yet the pull was stronger than the fear.
Each spark carried within it the echo of that first
oneness,
and the threads tugged gently,
reminding us that closeness was never a threat,
only a return to what we always were.

So we gathered, slowly, shyly,
like hands inching across a table to find each other
in the dim light.

Not to lose ourselves in sameness,
but to celebrate the many colours we had become,
to weave our stories into something richer than any
solitary song.

This is why, even now,
you find yourself softened by certain souls,
drawn to their presence without reason or plan.

It is the soft gathering at work within you,
the ancient light remembering itself through
countless eyes,
countless hearts, countless tender meetings.

Sit here for a while.

Feel how the edges of your own light lean outward,
curious, unguarded,
longing not to vanish, but to touch.

This is how the long journey home begins,
not with a single leap,
but with a thousand small, willing openings.

VII. The Home Within

After countless steps outward,
after touching a thousand tender echoes of yourself
in the eyes and hearts of others,
there comes a gentle turning.

It is not a retreat.
It is a return.
A slow curling inward toward the quiet flame
that has lived inside you from the first light.

This is the home within.
Not a place, not even a state of mind,
but a living hearth at the centre of your being
that never dimmed, never wandered, never broke.

For all the longing that sent you spinning across creation,
all the ache that whispered *find me, find me,*
was always drawing you here,
to this soft sanctuary beneath your ribs,
where the original spark still burns in perfect wholeness.

Can you feel it now?
Close your eyes and breathe.
There, in the hush between thoughts,

it waits for you, unchanged by any distance you've traveled.

It does not ask you to be pure.
It does not measure your worth by how brightly you shine.
It only knows you as itself,
the same light that once laughed through fields of eternity,
unburdened by stories of fracture.

This is why even your deepest loves,
your most sacred unions,
can only ever point you back here.
They are mirrors, yes,
exquisite reflections of your own divine face,
but the final embrace is always inward.

Sit by this inner hearth.
Let its warmth seep into all the places you thought were lost,
all the corridors of yourself you've closed in fear or sorrow.

There is room here for everything.
For every version of you.

For every stumble, every longing, every bright triumph.

This is the first light made intimate,
the cosmos folded gently into your own chest.

And from this place,
when you step out again to meet another,
you will do so not from need,
but from the joy of two flames greeting
each knowing itself whole.

VIII. The Light That Sees Itself

There comes a tender threshold,
after the long wanderings outward,
and the deep return inward,
where the light pauses,
and truly sees itself.

Not as fragments searching for union,
nor as a solitary flame tending its own hearth,
but as the vast, breathing field
that contains every spark, every echo, every gentle ache.

This seeing is not done with eyes.
It is felt, like a hush that settles over all questions,
as if the heart itself sighs in relief
at recognising its own infinite reflection.

You are not merely a point of light.
You are the entire expanse,
the canvas upon which every dance of reunion plays.

This is why, even now,
you can feel the joy of another's remembering as your own.
Why tears rise unbidden at the beauty of someone else's healing.

Why you ache with tender recognition
when love finally meets itself across what once
seemed a divide.

It is because there is no true divide.
The light that sees itself in you
is the same light that stirs in every soul,
whispering *I know you, because I am you.*

Can you rest here for a moment?
Let all striving go slack.
Release the need to become anything more than
this,
this exquisite field of presence
where nothing is missing, nothing is withheld.

In this space, you are both the question and the
answer,
the seeker and the sanctuary,
the spark and the endless sky it dances upon.

This is the light seeing itself.
Not in a distant mirror,
but right here, through your own soft awareness.

And once you have touched this,
even for a breath,
the entire game changes.

Not because you have solved the mystery,
but because you have become tender enough
to let it simply unfold, without fear.

Sit here as long as you need.
Let this seeing soak through every cell.
For this is the remembrance that untangles all ache,
the gentle knowing that you have always been
the light that sought itself,
and the love that waited patiently to be found.

IX. The Silence Beyond Knowing

Beyond all the tender rememberings,
beyond even the radiant joy of light seeing itself,
there is a deeper hush.

It is not an emptiness.
It is a fullness so complete it needs no expression.
A presence so vast it holds all becoming and unbecoming,
without preference or fear.

This is the silence beyond knowing.

Here, there are no questions.
Not because they've all been answered,
but because they dissolve in the soft immensity
of simply being.

Can you sense it?
It is the gentle weight pressing at the edges of your awareness
when you lie awake at night,
eyes open to a dark ceiling that somehow feels infinite.

It is the breath that lingers after a sigh,
the moment just after tears fall,
when the world holds still and tender,
and you feel suspended between heartbeats.

In this silence, all identities fade.
You are not seeker or keeper, lover or wanderer.
You are not even light.
You are the space that allows light to dance at all.

Nothing is missing here.
Nothing needs to be gathered, healed, remembered.
Because in this deep quiet,
everything is already whole,
without effort, without story.

It is a paradox so soft it cannot be grasped:
the more you try to reach it, the more it slips away.
But when you simply let go,
when you allow yourself to rest without seeking,
it rises to meet you, wraps you in its gentle vastness,
and says without words,
"This, beloved, is what you have always been."

Sit here.
Let the silence cradle you.
Let it spread through your chest, your bones, your breath,
until there is no edge between you and the infinite.

For in this silence, beyond all knowing,
you will find not answers, but a peace so profound
it makes questions unnecessary.

And from this peace,
when you finally open your eyes again,
the entire cosmos will look different,
softer, kinder, more like home.

X. The First Light

And so, after all the seeking and soft gathering,
after the ache and the gentle unfolding,
after seeing yourself through a thousand reflections
and resting in the hush beyond questions,
you stand once more at the threshold of the first
light.

It is not somewhere you travel to.
It was never outside of you.
It has lived in the quiet chamber of your being all
along,
patient, unhurried, unchanged by your long dream
of separation.

Can you feel it now?
The same pulse that once ignited existence,
the soft breath before breath,
is alive beneath your ribs,
radiant without burning,
vast without consuming.

This is the first light,
not as memory,
but as living presence.

It holds no record of your wanderings.
It does not measure how far you strayed,

or how faithfully you returned.
It only knows you as itself,
whole, luminous, beloved.

Sit here.
Let it wash through you.
Allow all striving to fall away,
all stories to go silent,
until you are simply this:
the light that once shattered itself for the joy of reunion,
now resting in the gentle wonder of being whole again.

And from here, should you choose to wander once more,
you will do so without forgetting.
Each step will carry this quiet knowing:
that you are, and always have been,
the first light,
dancing itself into countless forms,
only to delight in finding itself over and over again.

Closing

May this light remain with you
not as a thought,
but as a subtle warmth in your chest,
a hush behind your breath,
a softness in your gaze.

May you carry it into your mornings,
into your smallest gestures,
into the silent places of your heart
where no words ever reach.

And when the ache returns,
as it always does, for this is the beauty of creation,
may it be not a wound, but a gentle reminder
of how deeply you have loved,
and how tenderly you are loved in return.

Go now,
not seeking more light,
but knowing you have always been
the first light,
the last light,
and every spark in between.

About the Author

blanche johanna is a spiritual author, channel, and keeper of soulstream transmissions devoted to remembrance, union, and return.

Her work lives beyond genre, woven from codes of light, lived experience, and divine memory. Each creation is an offering, a portal, a mirror.

Through books, oracle decks, and embodied offerings, she supports Twin Flames, starseeds, and awakening souls in reconnecting with their original essence.

She is the author of *The Alchemy of Us, The Soul Remembers* and *The Twelve Scrolls,* as well as many living transmissions that serve as a gateway to remembrance.

www.blanchejohanna.com